Pattern making &
Garment construction

DRAFTED by
Alamu kumarappan

&

Thamarai pravin doss

Table of contents:

20	Kattori 2 blouse	103
21	Six piece saree petticoat	110
22	Fish cut saree petticoat	114
23	Full nighty	118
24	Full gown	125
25	Formal pant	129
26	Cigarette pant	134
27	Pallazzo pant	139
28	Formal shirt	145
29	Gagra skirt	153
30	Choli/crop top	157

JABLA

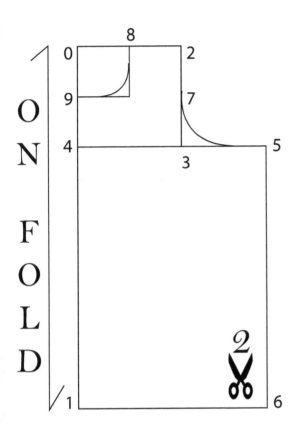

Fabrics Required:

kind of fabric = cotton (any kids print)

Infant= 30cms

Toddler = 0.5 mt

Measurements for Infant:

FULL LENGTH: 12"

SHOULDER: 8"

CHEST: 18"

DRAFTING PROCEDURE:

(0 - 1) = Full length + Seam allowance (1.5")

(0 - 2) = 1/2 Shoulder

(2 - 3) = 1/2 Shoulder

(0 - 4) = Same as (2 - 3)

(4 - 5) = 1/4 chest + 0.5" (ease) +1.5" (S.A)

Square down from 5 and 1. mark 6

find the mid point for (2 - 3) name it 7

draw a curve line for (2 - 7 - 5)

(0 - 8) = 1/12 chest + 1" (S. A)

(0 - 9) = 1/8 chest (front neck) + 0. 25" (S . A)

Stitching Flow Chart:

Step 1: Cross piece joining

Step 2: Finish front and back neck with cross piece

Step 3: Side joining

Step 4: Finish arm hole with cross piece

Step 5: Bottom hemming

A-LINE FROCK

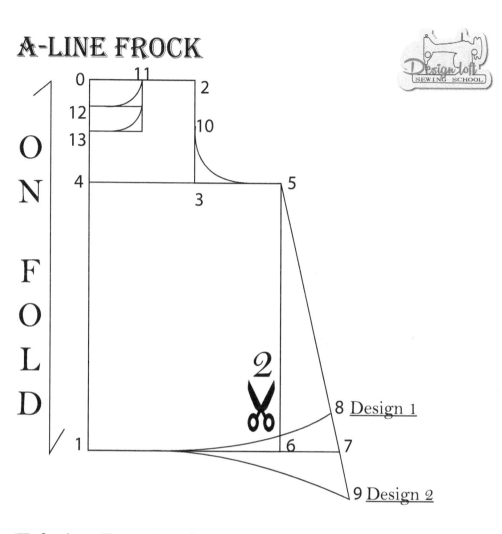

Fabrics Required:
Kind of fabric = cotton
Infant = 0.5mts
Toddler = 1mts
Kids = 1.5mts

A-LINE FROCK

Measurements for Toddler:

FULL LENGTH: 22"

SHOULDER: 9.5"

CHEST: 24"

DRAFTING PROCEDURE:

(0 - 1) = Full length + Seam allowance 1.5"(S . A)

(0 - 2) = 1/2 Shoulder

(2 - 3) = 1/2 Shoulder

(0 - 4) = Same as (2 - 3)

(4 - 5) = 1/4 chest + 0.5" (ease) +1.5" (S . A)

Square down from 5 and 1. mark 6

(6 - 7) = 3" for Flare

(7 - 8) = 1 " for shape (Design 1)
join (1 - 8) with a curve line

(7 - 9) = 3" for shape (Design 2)
join (1 - 9) with a curve line

find the mid point for (2 - 3) name it 10

draw a curve line for (2 - 10 - 5)

(0 - 11) = 1/12 chest (neck open)

(0 - 12) = 1/12 chest (Back neck) + 0. 25 (S . A)

(0 - 13) = 1/8 chest (front neck) + 0. 25 (S . A)

Stitching Flow Chart:

Step 1: Finish the neck and arm with the block piece

↓

Step 2: Shoulder joining

↓

Step 3: Side joining

↓

Step 4: Bottom hemming

WAIST FROCK
Yoke:

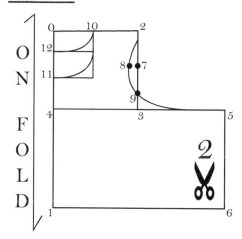

Skirt:

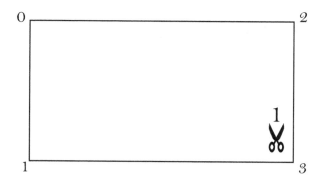

Fabrics Required:

Kind of fabric = cotton,rayan cotton

Toddler = Yoke : 0.5mts/ Skirt : 1mts

Kids = Yoke :0.5mts – 1mts / Skirt : 1.5mts

WAIST FROCK

Measurements for 1year to 2 year kid:

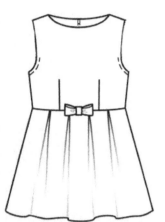

FULL LENGTH:24"

SHOULDER:10"

CHEST:24"

SEAT:26"

WAIST:24"

WAIST LENGTH:8"

SKIRT LENGTH:12"

FRONT NECK:3.5"

BACK NECK2.5"

DRAFTING PROCEDURE:

Yoke:

(0 - 1) = waist length + Seam allowance (1.5")

(0 - 2) = 1/2 Shoulder

(2 - 3) (0 - 4) = 1/2 Shoulder

(4 - 5) = 1/4 chest + 0.5" (ease) +1.5" (S.A)

(1 - 6) = 1/4 waist + Seam allowance

Arm :

7 is the mid point of (2- 3)

(8 - 7) = 0.25"

(3 - 9) = 1"

Neck :

(0 - 10) = 1/12 chest (Neck open)

(0 - 11) = Front neck + Seam allowance (0.25")

(0 - 12) = Back neck + Seam allowance (0.25")

Skirt:

(0 - 1) = Full length - Waist length +
         (1.5") Seam allowance

(0 - 2) = Fabric width/ 3 times of Seat

Square down from 2 and 1 mark 3

Stitching Flow Chart:

Step 1: Pleats arrangements on skirt fabric

Step 2: Finish the neck and arm with block piece

Step 3: Shoulder joining

Step 4: Skirt attachment to front and back piece

Step 5: Sides joining

Step 6: Bottom hemming

CIRCULAR SKIRT

1

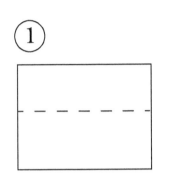

2 ON FOLD

2 Layers

3 ON FOLD

ON FOLD

4 Layers

4

ON FOLD

ON FOLD

8 Layers

CIRCULAR SKIRT

8 Layers:

4 Layers:

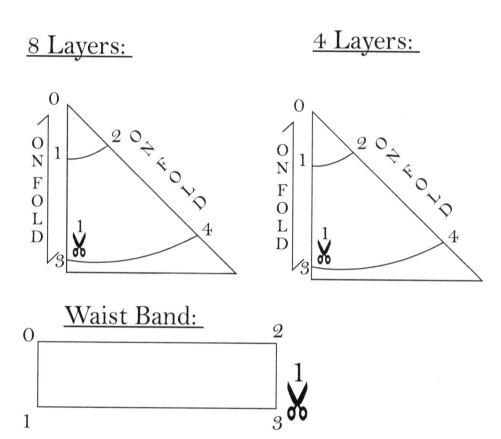

Waist Band:

Fabrics Required:

Kind of fabric = cotton,rayan cotton,synthetic silk,printed fabrics, crushed cotton

Toddler = 1mts

Kids = 1.5 - 3 mts

14

CIRCULAR SKIRT

Measurements :

LENGTH: 15"

WAIST: 22"

WAIST BAND LENGTH: 2"

DRAFTING PROCEDURE:

(0 - 1) = 1/6 Waist (for 8 layers),
1/4 waist (for 4 layers) + S.A

(0 - 2) = Same as (0 - 1)

(1 - 3) = Skirt Length + S.A

(2 - 4) = Same as (1 - 3)

Waist Band:

(0 - 1) = Waist band length + Seam allowance (3")

(0 - 2) = Waist + Seam allowance (1")

Square down from 2 and 1 mark 3

Stitching Flow Chart:

Step 1: Waist band attachment

Step 2: Elastic insert

Step 3: Bottom hemming

PAVADAI & CHATTAI

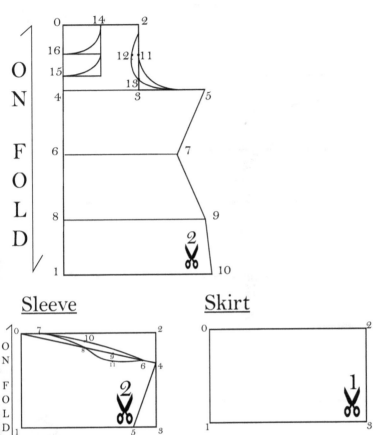

Sleeve

Skirt

Fabrics Required:

Kind of fabric = cotton,silk cotton,silk,
raw silk, Malai silk,chanderi silk

Toddler = Shirt : 0.5mts/ Skirt : 1mts

Kids = Shirt :0.5mts - 1mts / Skirt : 1.5 - 3mts

PAVADAI & CHATTAI

Measurements:

SKIRT LENGHTH:

SHOULDER:

CHEST:

WAIST:

WAIST LENGTH:

FRONT NECK:

BACK NECK:

SLEEVE LENGTH:

SLEEVE OPEN:

ARM ROUND:

SKIRT LENGTH:

SEAT:

DRAFTING PROCEDURE:

$(0 - 1) =$ Shirt length + Seam allowance(1.5")

$(0 - 2) = 1/2$ Shoulder

$(2 - 3)(0 - 4) = 1/2$ Shoulder

$(4 - 5) = 1/4$ chest + 0.5" (Ease allowance) + 1.5" (S.A)

$(0 - 6) =$ Waist length

$(6 - 7) = 1/4$ waist + 1.5" Seam allowance

$(6 - 8) = 5"$

$(8 - 9) = 1/4$ Seat + 1" Seam allowance

$(1 - 10) = (8 - 9)$

18

Arm :

11 is the mid point of (2- 3)

(11 - 12) = 0.25"

(3 - 13) = 1"

Join (2 -11 - 5) for back

(2 - 12 - 13 - 5) for front

Neck :

(0 - 14) = 1/12 chest (Neck open)

(0 - 15) = Front neck + Seam allowance (0 .25")

(0 - 16) = Back neck + Seam allowance (0.25")

Sleeve:

(0 -1) = Sleeve length + Seam allowance (1.5")

(0 -2) = Arm round\ 2 + 1"

Square down from 2 and 1 and mark 3

(2 - 4) = 1/12 chest

(1 - 5) = Half Sleeve Open +
Seam allowance (1.5")

Draw a line for (0 - 4)

(4 - 6) = 1.5"

(0 - 7) = 1"

8 is the mid point of (0 - 6)

9 is the mid point of (8 - 6)

(8 - 10) is 0.5" above

(9 - 11) is 0.25" below

Join (0 - 7 - 10 - 6 - 4) Back shape

(0 -7 - 8 - 11 - 6 - 4) Front shape

Skirt:

(0 - 1) = Full length - Waist length + Seam allowance

(0 - 2) = Fabric width/ 3 times of Seat

Square down from 2 and 1 mark 3

Stitching Flow Chart: Skirt:

Step 1: Tuck stitching

Step 2: Pleats arrangements

Step 3: Neck and arm finish for the body piece

Step 4: Placket on Back of the body piece

Step 5: Attach the skirt to the body piece, and join the sides

Shirt:

Step 1: Front and back neck finish with block /cross piece

Step 2: Back placket

Step 3: Shoulder join

Step 4: Sleeve hemming

Step 5: Sleeve join

Step 6: Front and back dart

Step 7: Side joining

Step 8: Bottom and side finish

Step 9: Hook and eye stitching

KURTHA W/O LINING

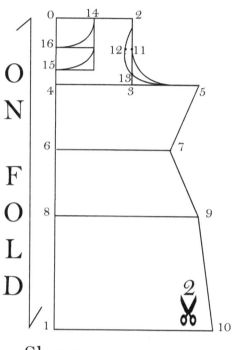

Sleeve:

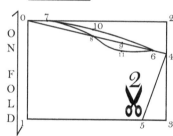

Fabrics Required:
Kind of fabric = Cotton

XS - S = 2mts

M - L = 2.5mts

XL - XXL = 3mts

KURTHA W/O LINING

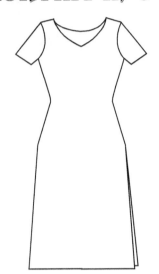

Measurements

FULL LENGTH:

SHOULDER:

CHEST:

WAIST LENGTH:

WAIST:

SEAT:

FRONT NECK:

BACK NECK:

SLEEVE LENGTH:

SLEEVE OPEN:

ARM ROUND:

DRAFTING PROCEDURE:

(0 - 1) = Full length + Seam allowance (1.5")

(0 - 2) = 1/2 Shoulder

(2 - 3) (0 - 4) = 1/2 Shoulder

(4 - 5) = 1/4 chest + 0.5" (Ease allowance) + 1.5" (S.A)

(0 - 6) = Waist length

(6 - 7) = 1/4 waist + 1.5" Seam allowance

(6 - 8) = 6"

(8 - 9) = 1/4 Seat + 1" Seam allowance

(1 - 10) = (8 - 9) + 0.5"

Arm :

11 is the mid point of (2- 3)

(11 - 12) = 0.25"

(3 - 13) = 1"

Join (2 -11 - 5) for back & (2 - 12 - 13 - 5) for front

Neck :

(0 - 14) = 1/12 chest (Neck open)

(0 - 15) = Front neck + Seam allowance (0.25")

(0 - 16) = Back neck + Seam allowance (0.25")

Sleeve:

(0 -1) = Sleeve length + Seam allowance (1.5")

(0 -2) = Arm round\ 2 + 1"

Square down from 2 and 1 and mark 3

(2 - 4) = 1/12 chest

(1 - 5) = Half Sleeve Open + Seam allowance (1.5")

Draw a line for (0 – 4)

(4 - 6) = 1.5"

(0 - 7) = 1"

8 is the mid point of (0 - 6)

9 is the mid point of (8 - 6)

(8 - 10) is 0.5" above

(9 - 11) is 0.25" below

Join (0 - 7 - 10 - 6 - 4) Back shape

(0 -7 - 8 - 11 - 6 - 4) Front shape

Stitching Flow Chart:

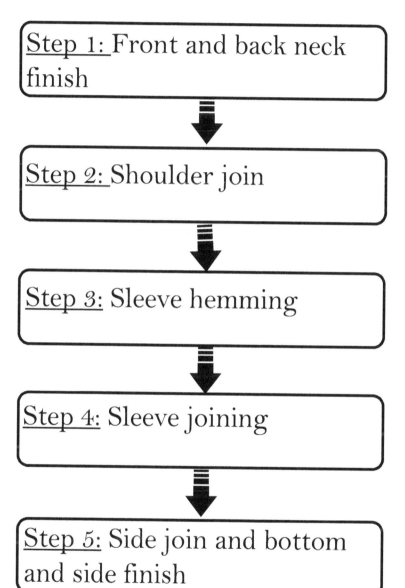

Step 1: Front and back neck finish

Step 2: Shoulder join

Step 3: Sleeve hemming

Step 4: Sleeve joining

Step 5: Side join and bottom and side finish

KURTHA WITH LINING

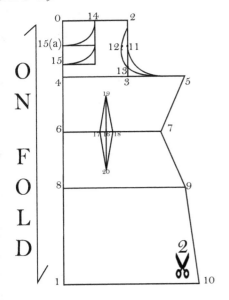

__Sleeve__

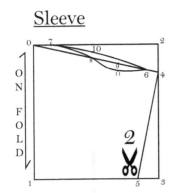

Fabrics Required:

Kind of fabric = Chanderi cotton, any silk mix material

XS - S = 2mts

M - L = 2.5mts

XL - XXL = 3mts

KURTHA WITH LINING

Measurements

FULL LENGTH:
SHOULDER:
CHEST:
WAIST:
WAIST LENGTH:
SEAT:
FRONT NECK:
BACK NECK:
SLEEVE LENGTH:
SLEEVE OPEN:
ARM ROUND:

DRAFTING PROCEDURE:

$(0 - 1) =$ Full length + Seam allowance

$(0 - 2) = 1/2$ Shoulder

$(0 - 2) = 1/2$ shoulder - 1.5"
Note: Only when both the neck measurement is more than 4"

$(2 - 3)(0 - 4) = 1/2$ Shoulder

$(4 - 5) = 1/4$ chest + 0.5" (Ease allowance) + 1.5" (S.A)

$(0 - 6) =$ Waist length

$(6 - 7) = 1/4$ waist + 1.5" Seam allowance

$(6 - 8) = 6"$

$(8 - 9) = 1/4$ Seat + 1" Seam allowance

$(1 - 10) = (8 - 9) + 0.5"$

Arm :

11 is the mid point of (2- 3)

(11 - 12) = 0.25"   Join (2 -11 - 5) for back

(3 - 13) = 1"   (2 - 12 - 13 - 5) for front

Neck :

(0 - 14) = 1/12 chest (Neck open)

(0 - 15) = Front neck + Seam allowance (0.25")

(0 - 15(a)) = Back neck + Seam allowance (0.25")

Dart:

(6 - 16) is 4" from waist for Back
and 3.5" from waist for Front

(17 - 18) is 1"

16 is the mid point of (17 - 18)

(16 - 19) is 4"

(16 - 20) is 5"

Join (19 - 17 - 20) (19 - 18 - 20)

Sleeve:

(0 -1) = Sleeve length + Seam allowance (1.5")

(0 -2) = Arm round\ 2 + 1"

Square down from 2 and 1 and mark 3

(2 - 4) = 1/12 chest

(1 - 5) − Half Sleeve Open + Seam allowance (1.5")

Draw a line for (0 - 4)

(4 - 6) = 1.5"

(0 - 7) = 1"

8 is the mid point of (0 - 6)

9 is the mid point of (8 - 6)

(8 - 10) is 0.5" above

(9 - 11) is 0.25" below

Join (0 - 7 - 10 - 6 - 4) Back shape

(0 -7 - 8 - 11 - 6 - 4) Front shape

Stitching Flow Chart:

Step 1: Front and back neck finish using cross piece/ block

Step 2: Shoulder join

Step 3: Sleeve hand hemming

Step 4: Sleeve attachment

Step 5: Dart on the back piece

<u>Step 6:</u> Side joining

<u>Step 7:</u> Bottom and side finish

PRINCESS CUT TOP

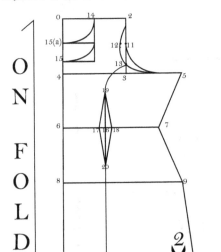

Sleeve:

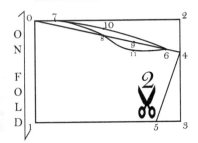

Fabrics Required:

Kind of fabric = Printed Cotton, Rayan cotton

XS - S = 2mts

M - L = 2.5mts

XL - XXL = 3mts

PRINCESS CUT TOP

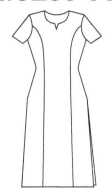

Measurements

FULL LENGTH:
SHOULDER:
CHEST:
WAIST LENGTH:
WAIST:
SEAT:
FRONT NECK:
BACK NECK:
SLEEVE LENGTH:
SLEEVE OPEN:
ARM ROUND:

DRAFTING PROCEDURE:

(0 - 1) = Full length + Seam allowance

(0 - 2) = 1/2 Shoulder

(0 - 2) = 1/2 shoulder - 1.5"
Note: Only when both the neck measurement is more than 4"

(2 - 3) (0 - 4) = 1/2 Shoulder

(4 - 5) = 1/4 chest + 0.5" (Ease allowance) + 1.5" (S.A)

(0 - 6) = Waist length

(6 - 7) = 1/4 waist + 1.5" Seam allowance

(6 - 8) = 6"

(8 - 9) = 1/4 Seat + 1" Seam allowance

(1 - 10) = (8 - 9) + 0.5"

Arm :

11 is the mid point of (2- 3)

(11 - 12) = 0.25"   Join (2 -11 - 5) for back

(3 - 13) = 1"   (2 - 12 - 13 - 5) for front

Neck :

(0 - 14) = 1/12 chest (Neck open)

(0 - 15) = Front neck + Seam allowance (0.25")

(0 - 15 (a)) = Back neck + Seam allowance (0.25")

Dart:

(6 - 16) is 4" from waist for back
and 3.5" from waist for front
(17 - 18) is 1"

16 is the mid point of (17 - 18)

(16 - 19) is 4"

(16 - 20) is 5"

Join (19 - 17 - 20) (19 - 18 - 20)
Draw a curve line from (13 - 19) and extend the line to 21

Sleeve:

(0 -1) = Sleeve length + Seam allowance (1.5")

(0 -2) = Arm round\ 2 + 1"

Square down from 2 and 1 and mark 3

(2 - 4) = 1/12 chest

(1 - 5) = Half Sleeve Open + Seam allowance (1.5")

Draw a line for (0 - 4)

(4 - 6) = 1.5"

(0 - 7) = 1"

8 is the mid point of (0 - 6)

9 is the mid point of (8 - 6)

(8 - 10) is 0.5" above

(9 - 11) is 0.25" below

Join (0 - 7 - 10 - 6 - 4) Back shape

(0 -7 - 8 - 11 - 6 - 4) Front shape

Stitching Flow Chart:

Step 1: Join princess line

Step 2: Front and back neck finish using cross piece/block

Step 3: Shoulder join

Step 4: Sleeve hand hemming

Step 5: Sleeve attachment

Step 6: Side joining

Step 7: Bottom and side finish

CHUDI BOTTOM

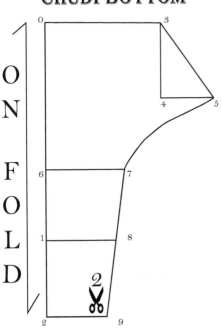

Waist band:

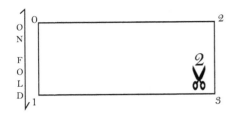

Fabrics Required:

Kind of fabric = Cotton, silk cotton

XS - S = 2mts

M - L = 2.5mts

XL - XXL = 3mts

CHUDI BOTTOM

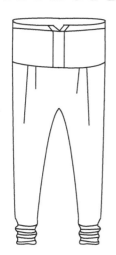

Measurements

FULL LENGTH:

WAIST:

SEAT:

KNEE LENGTH:

CALF ROUND:

BOTTOM OPEN:

KNEE ROUND:

DRAFTING PROCEDURE:

(0 -1) = Full length - Waist band

(1 - 2) = Gathers length (10")+ Seam allowance (1.5")

(0 - 3) = 1/4 Seat + 3" pleats + Seam allowance (1.5")

(3 - 4) = 1/4 seat / 1/6 Seat + Seam allowance (1.5")

(4 - 5) = 2" for shape

(0 - 6) = Knee length - Waist band

(6 - 7) = 1/2 Knee round + 1" Seam allowance

(1 - 8) = 1/2 bottom open + 1.5" Seam allowance

(2 - 9) = 1/2 bottom open + 1" Seam allowance

Waist band:

(0 -1) = Waist band length + Seam allowance

(0 - 2) = 1/4 Seat + 0.5" Ease allowance + 1" S.A

Square down from 2 and 1 and name it as 3

Stitching Flow Chart:

Step 1: Pleat arrangement to waist band width

Step 2: Waist band attachment

Step 3: Stitch nada loop

Step 4: Bottom hemming

Step 5: Bottom placket for hook and eye and side join

SALWAR BOTTOM

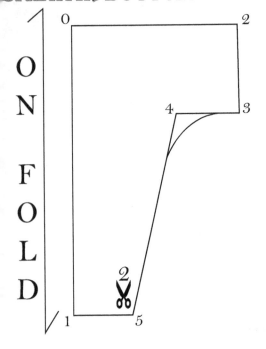

Waist band:

Fabrics Required:

Kind of fabric = Cotton

XS - S = 2mts

M - L = 2.5mts

XL - XXL = 3mts

SALWAR BOTTOM

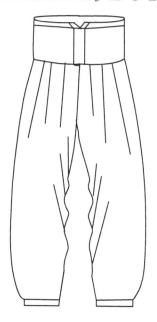

Measurements

FULL LENGTH:

WAIST BAND LENGTH : 7"

SEAT:

BOTTOM OPEN:

DRAFTING PROCEDURE:

(0 - 1) = Full length - Waist band + S.A

(0 - 2) = 1/2 Seat

(2 - 3) = 1/4 Seat + S.A (Seat above 40")
        1/6 Seat (Seat below 40")

(3 - 4) = 2" for shape

(1- 5) = 1/2 Bottom open + S.A

Join (4 - 5), draw a curve line to 3

Waist band:

(0 -1) = Waist band length + Seam allowance

(0 - 2) = 1/4 Seat + 0.5" Ease allowance + 1" S.A

Square down from 2 and 1 and name it as 3

Stitching Flow Chart:

> **Step 1:** Pleat arrangement to waist band width

> **Step 2:** Waist band attachment

> **Step 3:** Stitch nada loop

> **Step 4:** Bottom hemming with canvas

> **Step 5:** Side joining

SEMI PATIALLA

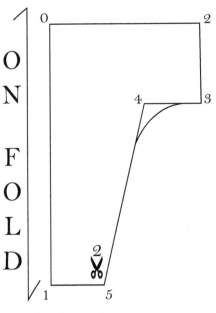

Waist band:

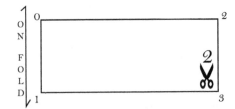

Fabrics Required:

Kind of fabric = Cotton, printed cotton, lissy bissy, san crepe

XS - S = 2.5mts

M - L = 3mts

XL - XXL = 4 mts

49

SEMI PATIALLA

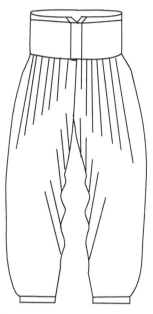

Measurements

FULL LENGTH:

WAIST BAND LENGTH: 7"

SEAT:

BOTTOM OPEN:

DRAFTING PROCEDURE:

(0 - 1) = Full length - Waist band + S.A

(0 - 2) = Fabric Width

(2 - 3) = 1/4 Seat + S.A (Seat above 40")
            1/6 Seat (Seat below 40")

(3 - 4) = 2" for shape

(1 - 5) = 1/2 Bottom open + S.A

Join (4 - 5) , draw a curve line to 3

not needed.

Waist band:

(0 -1) = Waist band length + Seam allowance

(0 - 2) = 1/4 Seat + 0.5 " Ease allowance + 1" S.A

Square down from 2 and 1 and name it as 3

Stitching Flow Chart:

Step 1: Pleat arrangement to waist band width

Step 2: Waist band attachment

Step 3: Stitch nada loop

Step 4: Bottom hemming with canvas

Step 5: Side joining

FULL PATIALLA

Panel 1

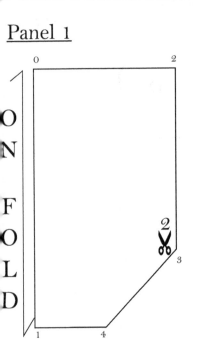

Panel 2

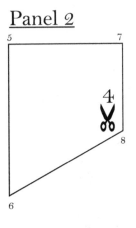

Panel 3

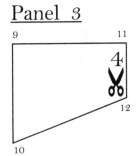

Waist band:

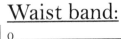

Fabrics Required:

Kind of fabric = Cotton , synthetic, san crepe

XS - S = 3mts - 4mts

M - L = 4mts - 5mts

XL - XXL = 5mts

FULL PATIALLA

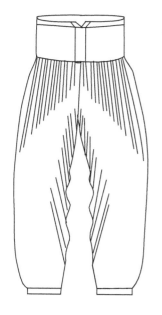

Measurements

FULL LENGTH:

WAIST:

SEAT:

BOTTOM OPEN:

DRAFTING PROCEDURE:

Diagram 1

(0 - 1) = Full length - Waist band + S.A

(0 - 2) = Fabric width

(2 - 3) = (0 - 1) - 10"

(1- 4) = 1/2 Bottom open + S.A

Diagram 2

(5 - 6) is same as (2 - 3)

(5 - 7) = Fabric width

(7 - 8) = (5 - 6) - 6"

Join (6 - 8)

Diagram 3

(9 - 10) is same as (7 - 8)

(9 - 11) = Fabric Width

(11 - 12) = 1/4 Seat + S.A (Seat above 40")
           1/6 Seat (Seat below 40")

Waist band:

(0 -1) = Waist band length + Seam allowance

(0 - 2) = 1/4 Seat + 0.5" Ease allowance + 1" S.A

Square down from 2 and 1 and name it as 3

Stitching Flow Chart:

Step 1: Attach panel 2 and 3 to panel 1 fabric on bothe sides

Step 2: Pleat arrangement to waist band width

Step 3: Waist band attachment

Step 4: Stitch nada loop

Step 5: Bottom hemming with canvas and Side joining

YOCK ANARKALLI TOP

Yoke:

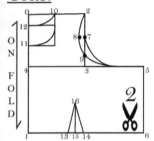

Front: **Back:**

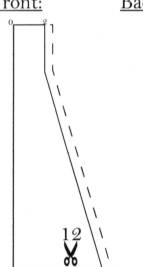
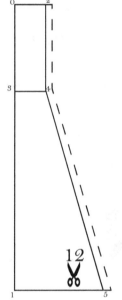

Fabrics Required:

Kind of fabric = Cotton, printed cotton, kalamkari cotton, ikat material

XS - S = Yoke - 1mts / kali - 2mts

M - L = Yoke - 1mts / Kali - 3mts

XL - XXL = 1.5mts / Kali - 4mts

YOCK ANARKALLI TOP

Measurements

FULL LENGTH:
SHOULDER:
CHEST:
WAIST:
SEAT:
FRONT NECK:
BACK NECK:
SLEEVE LENGTH:
SLEEVE OPEN:
ARM ROUND:
WAIST LENGTH:

DRAFTING PROCEDURE:

Yoke:

(0 - 1) = waist length + Seam allowance

(0 - 2) = 1/2 Shoulder

(0 - 2) = 1/2 shoulder - 1.5"
Note: Only when both the neck measurement is more than 4"

(2 - 3) (0 - 4) = 1/2 Shoulder

(4 - 5) = 1/4 chest + Ease allowance + Seam allowance

(1 - 6) = 1/4 waist + Seam allowance (1") + Dart 1"

Arm :

7 is the mid point of (2- 3)

(8 - 7) = 0.25"   Join (2 - 7 - 5) for back

(3 - 9) = 1"   (2 - 8 - 9 - 5) for front

Neck :
(0 - 10) = 1/12 chest (Neck open)

(0 - 11) = Front neck + Seam allowance (0.25")

(0 - 12) = Back neck + Seam allowance (0.25")

Front Panel: 24 panels
(0 - 1) = Full length - Waist length + Seam allowance (1.5")

(0 - 2) = 1/24 Waist + Seam allowance (0.5")

(1 - 3) = 3 Times of (0 - 2) + Seam allowance (0.5")
Note: Mark 1" extra from the panel measurement
for last 4 panels

Back Panel : For 24 panels:
(0 - 1) = Full length + Seam allowance (1.5")

(0 - 2) = 1/24 chest + Seam allowance (0.5")

(0 - 3) = Waist length

(3- 4) = same as (0 - 2)

(1 - 5) = 3 times of (0 - 2) + Seam allowance (0.5")
Dart:
(1 - 13) = 4" (back) / 3.5" (front)

(13 - 14) = 1"
15 is the mid point of (13 -14) , (15 - 16) = 3"
Join (16 - 13) (16 - 14)

Stitching Flow Chart:

Step 1: Prepare contrast colour fabric for coard piping

Step 2: Join shoulders

Step 3: Finish front and back neck with the coard piping

Step 4: Dart stitching

Step 5: Join panels and make it as a skirt

Step 6: Attach skirt to the yoke

Step 7: Check measurements with kurtha pattern

Step 8: Side joining

Step 9: Bottom finish

ANARKALLI TOP

Front:

Sleeve:

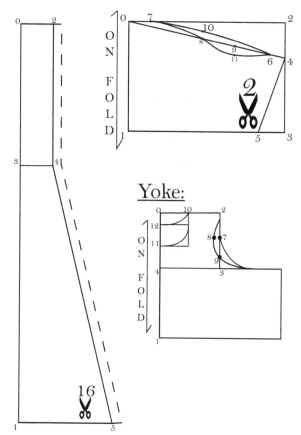

Yoke:

Fabrics Required:

Kind of fabric = Cotton

XS - S =

M - L =

XL - XXL =

ANARKALLI TOP

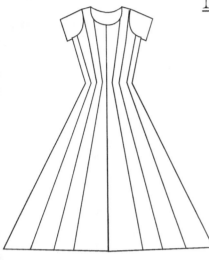

Measurements

FULL LENGTH:

SHOULDER:

CHEST:

WAIST:

SEAT:

FRONT NECK:

BACK NECK:

SLEEVE LENGTH:

SLEEVE OPEN:

ARM ROUND:

WAIST LENGTH:

DRAFTING PROCEDURE:

Panel : For 16 Panels

(0 - 1) = Full length + Seam Allowance(2")

(0 - 2) = 1/16 Chest + Seam allowance (0.5")

(1 - 5) = 3 Times of (0 - 2)

(0 - 3) = Waist Length

(3 - 4) = Is same as (0 - 2)

Note: Mark 1" extra from the panel measurement for last 4 panels

<u>yoke</u>:

(0 – 1) = waist length + Seam allowance(1")

(0 – 2) = 1/2 Shoulder

(2 – 3) (0 – 4) = 1/2 Shoulder

(4 – 5) = 1/4 chest + Seam allowance (1.5")

(1 – 6) = 1/4 waist + Seam allowance (1.5")

<u>Arm</u> :

7 is the mid point of (2– 3)

(8 – 7) = 0.25"

(3 – 9) = 1"

<u>Neck</u> :

(0 – 10) = 1/12 chest (Neck open)

(0 – 11) = Front neck + Seam allowance (0.25")

(0 – 12) = Back neck + Seam allowance (0.25")

<u>Sleeve</u>:

(0 –1) = Sleeve length + Seam allowance (1.5")

(0 –2) = Arm round\ 2 + 1"

Square down from 2 and 1 and mark 3

$(2 - 4) = 1 / 12$ chest

$(1 - 5) =$ Half Sleeve Open + Seam allowance (1.5")

Draw a line for (0 – 4)

$(4 - 6) = 1.5"$

$(0 - 7) = 1"$

8 is the mid point of (0 - 6)

9 is the mid point of (8 - 6)

(8 - 10) is 0.5" above

(9 - 11) is 0.25" below

Join (0 - 7 - 10 - 6 - 4) Back shape

(0 -7 - 8 - 11 - 6 - 4) Front shape

Stitching Flow Chart:

Step 1: Join panels

Step 2: Check measurements with kurtha pattern and cut

Step 3: finish front and back neck with cross piece/lining

Step 4: Shoulder join

Step 5: Sleeve joining

Step 6: Side joining

Step 7: Bottom joining

UMBERALLA TOP WITH COLLAR/PIPING

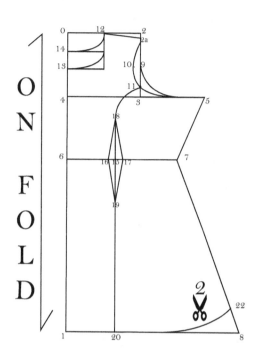

Sleeve:

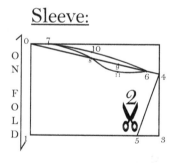

Collar

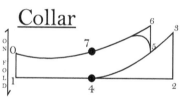

Fabric required

Kind of fabric = Cotton, rayan cotton

XS - S = 2.5mts

M - L = 3mts

XL - XXL = 3.5mts

UMBERALLA TOP WITH COLLAR/PIPING

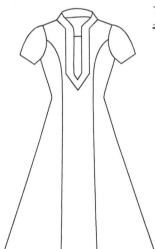

Measurements

FULL LENGTH:

SHOULDER:

CHEST:

WAIST:

SEAT:

FRONT NECK:

BACK NECK:

SLEEVE LENGTH:

SLEEVE OPEN:

ARM ROUND:

WAIST LENGTH:

DRAFTING PROCEDURE:

(0 - 1) = Full length + Seam allowance (1.5")

(0 - 2) = 1/2 Shoulder + Seam allowance (0.5")

(2 - 3) (0 - 4) = 1/2 Shoulder + 1"

(2 - 2a) = 1" for shoulder slope

(4-5) = 1/4 chest + 0.5" (ease) +1.5" (S.A)

(0 - 6) = Waist length

(6 - 7) = 1/4 waist + 1.5" Seam allowance

(1 - 8) = Fabric width

Arm :

9 is the mid point of (2- 3)

(9 - 10) = 0.25"inch

(3 - 11) = 1" inch

Neck :

(0 - 12) = 1/12 chest (Neck open)

(0 - 13) = Front neck (1/12 chest) + Seam allowance (0.25")

(0 - 14) = 0.5" (Back neck)

Dart:

(6 - 16) is 4" inch from waist for back
and 3.5" inch from waist for front

(16 - 17) is 1"

15 is the mid point of (16 - 17)

(15 - 18) is 4"

(15 - 19) is 5"

Join (18 - 16 - 19) (18 - 17 - 19)

Draw a curve line from (18 - 11) and extend the line down
to 20

8 - 21) = 2"

Join (20 - 21) with a curve line

Sleeve:

(0 -1) = Sleeve length + Seam allowance (1.5")

(0 -2) = Arm round\ 2 + 1"

Square down from 2 and 1 and mark 3

(2 - 4) = 1/12 chest

(1 - 5) = Half Sleeve Open + Seam allowance (1.5")

Draw a line for (0 - 4)

(4 - 6) = 1.5"

(0 - 7) = 1"

8 is the mid point of (0 - 6)

9 is the mid point of (8 - 6)

(8 - 10) is 0.5" above   (9 - 11) is 0.25" below

Join (0 - 7 - 10 - 6 - 4) Back shape
(0 -7 - 8 - 11 - 6 - 4) Front shape

Collar

(0 - 1) = Collar Width (1.25")

(1 - 2) = Half neck Round

(2 - 3) = 2"

4 is the mid point of (1 - 2)

Draw a curve line for (4 - 3)

(1 - 5) is same as (1 - 2)

(5 - 6), (4 - 7) = Collar Width (1.25")

Join 0 - 7 - 6 - 5

Draw a shape line for (6 - 5)

Step 1: Prepare coard piping

Step 2: Join princess line with coard piping

Step 3: finish front neck design with coard piping

Step 4: Shoulder join

Step 5: Prepare collar to attach to finish the neck

Step 6: Sleeve joining

Step 7: Side joining

Step 8: Bottom hemming

NORMAL BLOUSE

Back

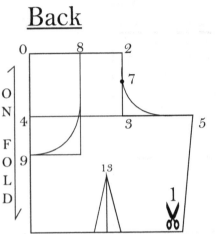

Front

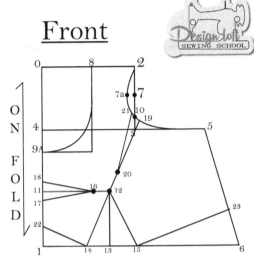

Patti:

Sleeve:

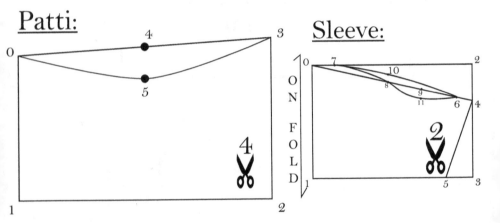

Fabrics Required:

Kind of fabric = Cotton, Printed cotton,
Kalamkari cotton

XS - S = 80cms

M - L = 90cms - 1mts

XL - XXL = 1.10mts - 1.5mts

NORMAL BLOUSE

MEASUREMENTS:

BLOUSE LENGTH:

SHOULDER:

CHEST:

WAIST:

FRONT NECK:

BACK NECK:

ARM ROUND:

SLEEVE LENGTH:

SLEEVE OPEN:

DART POINT:

DART WIDTH:

DRAFTING PROCEDURE:

<u>Back</u>:

(0 - 1) = Blouse length + Seam Allowance (1")

(0 - 2) = 1/2 Shoulder

(0 - 2) = 1/2 shoulder - 1.5"
Note: Apply Only when both the
neck measurement is more than 4"

(2 - 3) = 1/2 Shoulder - 1"

(0 - 4) = Same as (2 - 3)

(4 - 5) = 1/4 Chest + Ease allowance + Seam allowance (1.5")

(1 - 6) = 1/4 Waist + Dart (1") + Seam allowance (1.5")

Arm:

7 is the mid point of (2 - 3)

Draw a curve line for (2 - 7 - 5) Back Arm shape

Neck:

(0 - 8) = 1/12 Chest (Neck Open)

(0 - 9) = Back neck + Seam allowance (0.25")

Dart:

(1 - 10) = waist/8   12 is the mid point (10 - 11)

(10 - 11) = 1"   (12 - 13) = 3.5" .

Join (13 - 10) (13 - 11)

Front:

(0 - 1) = Dart point + 3.5"

(0 - 2) (2 - 3) (0 - 4) (4 - 5) (0 - 8)
 is Same as Back measurement

(1 - 6) = 1/4 Waist + Dart (3") + Seam allowance (1.5")

Neck:

(0 - 9a) = Front Neck + Seam allowance (0.25")

Arm:

(3 - 10) = 1"

(7 - 7a) = 0.25"

Draw a curve line for (2 - 7a - 10 - 5)

Dart:

(0 - 11) = Dart point

(11 - 12) = 1/2 Dart width

Square down from 11 and name as 13

(13 - 14), (13 - 15) = Each 1.5"

(12 - 16) = 1.5"

(11 - 17), (11 - 18) = 0.25" each

Join (17 - 16), (18 - 16)

Draw a diagonal line for (12 - 3) mark as 19

(12 - 20) - 2"

(19 - 21) = 0.5"   Join (21 - 20)

Shape:

(1- 22) = 1.5"

(6 - 23) = 2.5"

Join (22 - 14), (23 - 15)

Patti:

(0 - 1) = 5"

(1 - 2) = 1/4 Waist + 1" + Seam allowance (1.5")

(2 - 3) = 5.5", Join (0 -3)

4 is the mid point of (0 - 3)

(4 -5) = 1, Join (0 – 5 – 3) with a curve line

<u>Sleeve:</u>

(0 -1) = Sleeve length + Seam allowance(1.5")

(0 -2) = Arm round\ 2 + 1"

Square down from 2 and 1 and mark 3

(2 - 4) = 1/12 chest

(1 - 5) = Half Sleeve Open + Seam allowance (1.5")

Draw a line for (0 - 4)

(4 - 6) = 1.5"

(0 - 7) = 1"

8 is the mid point of (0 - 6)

9 is the mid point of (8 - 6)

(8 - 10) is 0.5" above   (9 - 11) is 0.25" below

Join (0 - 7 - 10 - 6 - 4) Back shape
(0 -7 - 8 - 11 - 6 - 4) Front shape

Stitching Flow Chart:

Step 1: Back piece bottom hemming

Step 2: Back dart finish

Step 3: front dart finish

Step 4: Shoulders join

Step 5: Patti attachment to front piece

Step 6: Patti bottom finish

Step 7: Front hook and eye placket

Step 8: Sleeve attachment

Step 9: Side join

Step 10: Front and back neck finish using cross piece

Step 11: Hook and eye stitching neck hemming

PRINCESS CUT 1 BLOUSE

Back

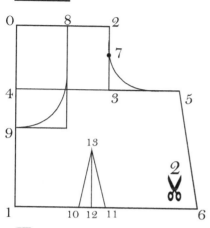

Front

Sleeve:

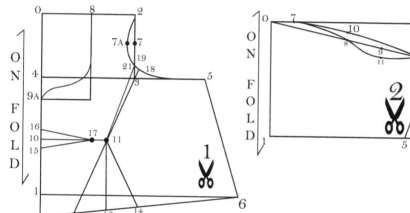

Fabrics Required:

Kind of fabric = Cotton, Printed cotton, Kalamkari cotton

XS - S = 90cms

M - L = 1mts

XL - XXL = 1.10mts - 1.5mts

PRINCESS CUT 1 BLOUSE:

MEASUREMENTS:

BLOUSE LENGTH:

SHOULDER:

CHEST:

WAIST:

FRONT NECK:

BACK NECK:

ARM ROUND:

SLEEVE LENGTH:

SLEEVE OPEN:

DART POINT:

DART WIDTH:

DRAFTING PROCEDURE:

Back:

(0 - 1) = Blouse length + Seam Allowance (1")

(0 - 2) = 1/2 Shoulder

(0 - 2) = 1/2 shoulder - 1.5"
Note: Apply Only when both the
neck measurement is more than 4"

(2 - 3) = 1/2 Shoulder - 1

(0 - 4) = Same as (2 - 3)

(4 - 5) = 1/4 Chest + Seam allowance

(1 - 6) = 1/4 Waist + Dart (1) + Seam allowance (1.5)

83

Arm:

7 is the mid point of (2 - 3)

Draw a curve line for (2 - 7 - 5) back arm shape

Neck:

(0 - 8) = 1/12 Chest (Neck open)

(0 - 9) = Back neck + Seam allowance (0.25")

Dart:

(1 - 10) = waist 1/8

(10 - 11) = 1"

12 is the mid point (10 - 11)

(12 - 13) = 3.5" .

Join (13 - 10) (13 - 11)

Front:

(0 - 1) = Blouse length + Seam allowance (1.5")

(0 - 2) (2 - 3) (0 - 4) (4 - 5) (0 - 8)
 is Same as Back measurement

(1 - 6) = 1/4 Waist + Dart (3") + Seam allowance (1.5")

(1 - 20) = 1" for shape   Join (6 - 20)

(0 - 9a) = Front neck + Seam allowance (0.25")

Dart:

(0 - 10) = Dart Point

(10 - 11) = 1/2 Dart width

Square down and mark as 12

(12 - 13) , (12 - 14) = Each 1.5"

Join (11 - 13) , (11 - 14)

(10 - 15) , (10 - 16) = 0.25"

(11 - 17) = 1.5'''

Join (16 - 17) , (15 - 17)

Draw a diagonal line for (11 - 18)

(18 - 19) = 0.5"

Join (19 - 11)

Arm:

(3 - 21) = 1"

(7 - 7a) = 0.25"

Draw a curve line for (2 - 7a - 21 - 5)

Sleeve:

(0 -1) = Sleeve length + Seam allowance (1.5")

(0 -2) = Arm round \ 2 + 1"

Square down from 2 and 1 and mark 3

(2 - 4) = 1/12 chest

(1 - 5) = Half Sleeve Open + Seam allowance (1.5")

Draw a line for (0 - 4)

(4 - 6) = 1.5"

(0 - 7) = 1"

8 is the mid point of (0 - 6)

9 is the mid point of (8 - 6)

(8 - 10) is 0.5" above   (9 - 11) is 0.25" below

Join (0 - 7 - 10 - 6 - 4) Back shape
(0 -7 - 8 - 11 - 6 - 4) Front shape

Stitching Flow Chart:

Step 1: Back placket for hook and eye

Step 2: Back hemming

Step 3: Back dart

Step 4: Princess cut joining

Step 5: Front middle dart

Step 6: Shoulder join

Step 7: Front bottom hemming

Step 8: Sleeve attachment

Step 9: Side join

Step 10: Front and back neck finish using cross piece/piping

Step 11: Hook and eye stitching neck hemming

Back

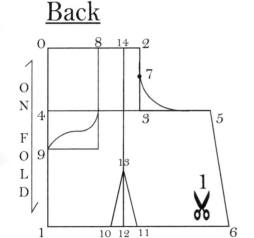

Front

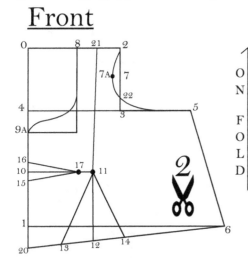

Sleeve:

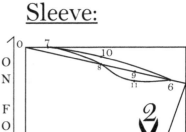

Fabrics Required:

Kind of fabric = Printed silk, silk cotton, net embroidery fabric, Banaras material

XS - S = 90cms

M - L = 1mts

XL - XXL = 1.10mts - 1.5mts

PRINCESS CUT 2 BLOUSE WITH SIDE ZIP

MEASUREMENTS:

BLOUSE LENGTH:

SHOULDER:

CHEST:

WAIST:

FRONT NECK:

BACK NECK:

ARM ROUND:

SLEEVE LENGTH:

SLEEVE OPEN:

DART POINT:

DART WIDTH:

DRAFTING PROCEDURE:

Back:

(0 - 1) = Blouse length + Seam Allowance (1")

(0 - 2) = 1/2 Shoulder

(0 - 2) = 1/2 shoulder - 1.5"
Note: Apply Only when both the
neck measurement is more than 4"

(2 - 3) = 1/2 Shoulder - 1"

(0 - 4) = Same as (2 - 3)

(4 - 5) = 1/4 Chest + Ease allowance + Seam allowance (1.5")

(1 - 6) = 1/4 Waist + Dart (1") + Seam allowance (1.5")

Arm:

7 is the mid point of (2 - 3)

Draw a curve line for (2 - 7 - 5) back arm shape

Neck:

(0 - 8) = 1/12 Chest (Neck open)

(0 - 9) = Back neck + Seam allowance (0.25")

Dart:

(1 - 10) = waist 1/8 | 12 is the mid point (10 - 11)

(10 - 11) = 1" | (12 - 13) = 3.5" .

Join (13 - 10) (13 - 11)

(8 - 2) = mid point is 14

join (13 -14) with the straight line

Front:

(0 - 1) = Blouse length + Seam allowance (1")

(0 - 2) (2 - 3) (0 - 4) (4 - 5) (0 - 8)
is Same as Back measurement

(1 - 6) = 1/4 Waist + Dart (3")+ Seam allowance (1.5")

(1 - 20) = 1" for shape   Join (6 - 20)

(0 - 9a) = Front neck + Seam allowance (0.25")

<u>Arm</u>:

(3 – 22) = 1"

(7 – 7a) = 0.25"

Draw a curve line for (2 – 7a – 22 – 5)

<u>Dart</u>:

(0 – 10) = Dart Point

(10 – 11) = 1/2 Dart width

Square down and mark as 12

(12 – 13) , (12 – 14) = Each 1.5"

Join (11 – 13) , (11 – 14)

(10 – 15) , (10 – 16) = 0.25"

(11 – 17) = 1"

Join (16 – 17) , (15 – 17)

(8 – 2) = mid point is 21

join (11 – 21) with the straight line

Sleeve:

(0 -1) = Sleeve length + Seam allowance (1.5")

(0 - 2) = Arm round\ 2 + 1"

Square down from 2 and 1 and mark 3

(2 - 4) = 1/12 chest

(1 - 5) = Half Sleeve Open + Seam allowance (1.5")

Draw a line for (0 - 4)

(4 - 6) = 1.5"

(0 - 7) = 1"

8 is the mid point of (0 - 6)

9 is the mid point of (8 - 6)

(8 - 10) is 0.5" above

(9 - 11) is 0.25" below

Join (0 - 7 - 10 - 6 - 4) Back shape

(0 -7 - 8 - 11 - 6 - 4) Front shape

Stitching Flow Chart:

Step 1: Princess cut joining on front and back

Step 2: Back neck finish

Step 3: Back hemming

Step 4: Front neck finish

Step 5: Front middle dart

Step 6: Shoulder join

Step 7: Front bottom hemming

Step 8: Sleeve attachment

Step 9: Side join

Step 10: Zip attachment

KATTORI 1 BLOUSE

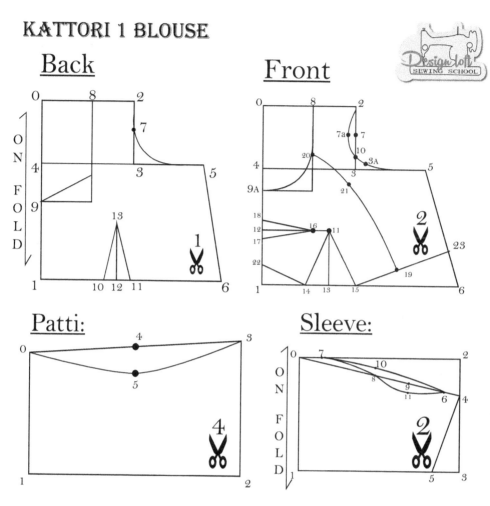

Fabrics Required:

Kind of fabric = Cotton, Printed cotton, Kalamkari cotton

XS - S = 90cms

M - L = 1mts

XL - XXL = 1.10mts - 1.5mts

KATTORI 1 BLOUSE

MEASUREMENTS:

BLOUSE LENGTH:
SHOULDERS:
CHEST:
WAIST:
FRONT NECK:
BACK NECK:
ARM ROUND:
SLEEVE LENGTH:
SLEEVE OPEN:
DART POINT:
DART WIDTH:

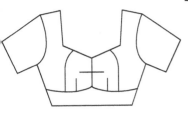

DRAFTING PROCEDURE:

Back:

(0 - 1) = Blouse length + Seam Allowance (1")

(0 - 2) = 1/2 Shoulder

(0 - 2) = 1/2 shoulder - 1.5"
Note: Apply Only when both the
neck measurement is more than 4"

(2 - 3) = 1/2 Shoulder - 1"

(0 - 4) = Same as (2 - 3)

(4 - 5) = 1/4 Chest + Seam allowance (1.5")

(1 - 6) = 1/4 Waist + Dart (1) + Seam allowance (1.5)

Arm:

7 is the mid point of (2 - 3)

Draw a curve line for (2 - 7 - 5) back arm shape

Neck:

(0 - 8) = 1/12 Chest (Neck)

(0 - 9 /0 = Back neck + Seam allowancec (0.25")

Dart:

(1 - 10) = Waist 1 /8   12 is the mid point (10 - 11)

(10 - 11) = 1"   (12 - 13) = 3.5" .

Join (13 - 10) (13 - 11)

Front:

(0 - 1) = Dart point + 3.5"

(0 - 2) (2 - 3) (0 - 4) (4 - 5) (0 - 8)
is Same as Back measurement

(1 - 6) = 1/4 Waist + Dart (3") + Seam allowance (1.5")

Neck:

(0 - 9a) = Front Neck + Seam allowance (0.25")

Arm:

(3 - 10) = 1"

(7 - 7a) = 0.25"

Draw a curve line for (2 - 7a - 10 - 5)

Dart:

(0 - 12) = Dart point

(12 - 11) = 1/2 Dart width

Square down from 11 and name as 13

(13 - 14), (13 - 15) = Each 1.5"

(11 - 16) = 1.5"

(12 - 7), (12 - 18) = 0.25" each

Join (17 - 16), (18 - 16)

(15 - 19) = 2"

20 = 1/2 of (8 - 9) + 1"

(3a - 21) = 1.5"

Join (19 - 21 - 20) with the curve line
Shape:
(1- 22) = 1.5"

(6 - 23) = 2"

Join (22 - 14), (23 - 15)

Patti:

(0 - 1) = 5"

(1 - 2) = 1/4 Waist + 1" + Seam allowance

2 - 3) = 5.5" , Join (0 -3)

4 is the mid point of (0 - 3)

(4 -5) = 1, Join (0 - 5 - 3) with a curve line

<u>Sleeve:</u>

(0 -1) = Sleeve length + Seam allowance (1.5")

(0 -2) = Arm round\ 2 + 1"

Square down from 2 and 1 and mark 3

(2 - 4) = 1/12 chest

(1 - 5) = Half Sleeve Open + Seam allowance (1.5")

Draw a line for (0 - 4)

(4 - 6) = 1.5"

(0 - 7) = 1"

8 is the mid point of (0 - 6)

9 is the mid point of (8 - 6)

(8 - 10) is 0.5" above   (9 - 11) is 0.25" below

Join (0 - 7 - 10 - 6 - 4) Back shape
(0 -7 - 8 - 11 - 6 - 4) Front shape

Stitching Flow Chart:

Step 1: Back hemming

Step 2: Back dart

Step 3: katori cut joining in the front

Step 4: Front dart and patti attachment

Step 5: Shoulder join

Step 6: Front patti

Step 7: Sleeve attachment

Step 8: Front hook and eye placket

Step 9: Side join

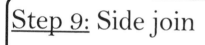

Step 10: Front and back neck finish using cross piece/piping

Step 11:Hook and eye stitching neck hemming

102

KATTORI 2 BLOUSE

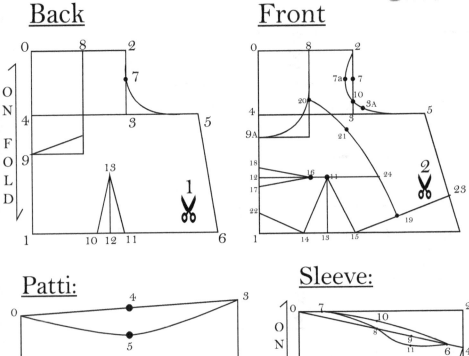

Fabrics Required:

Kind of fabric =Printed silk, silk cotton,
net embroidery fabric, Banaras material

XS - S = 90cms

M - L = 1mts

XL - XXL = 1.10mts - 1.5mts

KATTORI 2 BLOUSE

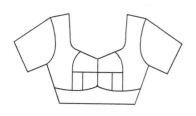

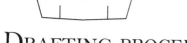

MEASUREMENTS:

BLOUSE LENGTH:

SHOULDERS:

CHEST:

WAIST:

FRONT NECK:

BACK NECK:

ARM ROUND:

SLEEVE LENGTH:

SLEEVE OPEN:

DART POINT:

DART WIDTH:

DRAFTING PROCEDURE:

Back

(0 - 1) = Blouse length + Seam Allowance (1")

(0 - 2) = 1/2 Shoulder

(0 - 2) = 1/2 shoulder - 1.5"
Note: Apply Only when both the
neck measurement is more than 4"

(2 - 3) = 1/2 Shoulder -1"

(0 - 4) = Same as (2 - 3)

(4 - 5) = 1/4 Chest + Seam allowance (1.5")

(1 - 6) = 1/4 Waist + Dart (1) + Seam allowance (1.5)

Arm:
7 is the mid point of (2 - 3)

Draw a curve line for (2 - 7 - 5) Back arm shape

Neck:
(0 - 8) = 1/12 Chest (Neck)

(0 - 9 /0 = Back neck + Seam allowance (0.25")

Dart:
(1 - 10) = Waist 1/8 $\qquad$ 12 is the mid point (10 - 11)

(10 - 11) = 1" $\qquad$ (12 - 13) = 3.5" .

Join (13 - 10) (13 - 11)

Front:
(0 - 1) = Dart point + 3.5"

(0 - 2) (2 - 3) (0 - 4) (4 - 5) (0 - 8)
is Same as Back measurement

(1 - 6) = 1/4 Waist + Dart (3") + Seam allowance (1.5")

Neck:
(0 - 9a) = Front Neck + Seam allowance (0.25")

Arm:
(3 - 10) = 1"
(7 - 7a) = 0.25"
Draw a curve line for (2 - 7a - 10 - 5)

Dart:

(0 - 12) = Dart point

(12 - 11) = 1/2 Dart width

Square down from 11 and name as 13

(13 - 14), (13 - 15) = Each 1.5"

(11 - 16) = 1.5"

(12 - 7), (12 - 18) = 0.25" each

Join (17 - 16), (18 - 16)

(15 - 19) = 2"

20 = 1/2 of (8 - 9) + 1"

(3a - 21) = 1.5"

Join (19 - 21 - 20) with the curve line

Extend the line from 11 and mark as 24

Shape:

(1- 22) = 1.5"

(6 - 23) = 2"

Join (22 - 14), (23 - 15)

Patti:
(0 - 1) = 5"

(1 - 2) = 1/4 Waist + 1" + Seam allowance
(2 - 3) = 5.5" , Join (0 -3)

4 is the mid point of (0 - 3)
(4 -5) = 1, Join (0 - 5 - 3) with a curve line

Sleeve:
(0 -1) = Sleeve length + Seam allowance (1.5")

(0 -2) = Arm round\ 2 + 1"

Square down from 2 and 1 and mark 3

(2 - 4) = 1/12 chest

(1 - 5) = Half Sleeve Open + Seam allowance (1.5")

Draw a line for (0 - 4)

(4 - 6) = 1.5"

(0 - 7) = 1"

8 is the mid point of (0 - 6)
9 is the mid point of (8 - 6)

(8 - 10) is 0.5" above   (9 - 11) is 0.25" below
Join (0 - 7 - 10 - 6 - 4) Back shape
(0 -7 - 8 - 11 - 6 - 4) Front shape

Stitching Flow Chart:

Step 1: Back hemming

Step 2: Back dart

Step 3: katori cut joining in the front

Step 4: Front dart and patti attachment

Step 5: Shoulder join

Step 6: Front patti

Step 7: Sleeve attachment

Step 8: Front hook and eye placket

Step 9: Side join

Step 10: Front and back neck finish using cross piece/piping

Step 11: Hook and eye stitching neck hemming

SIX PIECE SAREE PETTICOAT

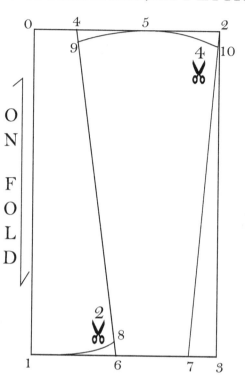

Waist band:

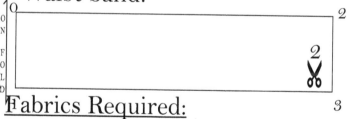

Fabrics Required:

Kind of fabric = Cotton, poplin,
Lace to decorate(Optional)

XS - S = 2mts

M - L = 2.5mts

XL - XXL = 3 - 3.5mts

SIX PIECE SAREE PETTICOAT

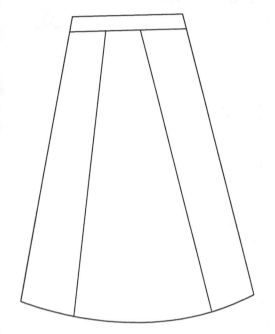

MEASUREMENTS:

FULL LENGTH:

WAIST:

SEAT:

DRAFTING PROCEDURE:

(0 - 1) = Full length

(0 - 2) = 1/2 Seat / fabric width

square down mark 3

(0 - 4) = 1/12 waist + 0.75" Seam allowance

5 = mid point of (4 - 2)

(1 - 6) = (4 - 5)

Join (6 - 4)

(6 - 7) = 2 times of (0 - 4)

join (7 - 2)

<u>shape</u>:

(6 - 8) (4 - 9) (2 - 10) each 1"

Join (1 - 8) (9 - 5) (5 - 10) with the curve lines

<u>Waist band</u>:

(0 - 1) = 5"

(0 - 2) = 1/4 of waist + Ease allowance + Seam allowance

Stitching Flow Chart:

Step 1: Pannels attachment

Step 2: Waist band attchments

Step 3: Nada loop

Step 4: Bottom hemming

FISH CUT SAREE PETTICOAT

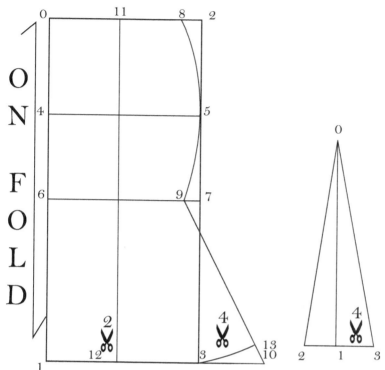

Waist band:

Fabrics Required:

Kind of fabric = Cotton, poplin,

Lace to decorate(Optional)

XS - S = 2mts

M - L = 2.5mts

XL - XXL = 3 - 3.5mts

FISH CUT SAREE PETTICOAT

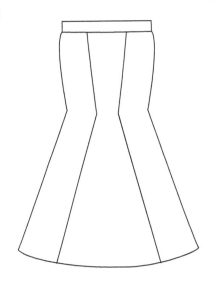

MEASUREMENTS:

FULL LENGTH:

WAIST:

SEAT:

DRAFTING PROCEDURE:

(0 - 1) = Full length

(0 - 2) = 1/4 Seat + Seam allowance

(2 - 3) = Square down

(0 - 4) = 7" for Seat line

(2 - 5) is same as (0 - 4)

(0 - 6) = 12"

(2 -7) is same as (0 - 6)

(0 - 8) = 1/4 Waist + Seam allowance

(7 - 9) = 1.5"

(3 - 10) = 4" for flare

Join 8 - 5 - 9 - 10 as shown in the diagram

mid point of (0 - 8) is 11

square down and mark 12

(10 - 13) is 1" for shape

Kalli:

(0 - 1) = (6 - 1) + 1"

(1 - 2) (1- 3) = 2.5" each

Join (0 - 2) (0 - 3)

Waist band:

(0 - 1) = 5"

(0 - 2) = 1/4 of waist + Ease allowance + Seam allowance

Stitching Flow Chart:

Step 1: " V" panel attachment

Step 2: Princess line joining

Step 3: Waist band joining

Step 4: Nada loop

Step 5: Bottom hemming

FULL NIGHTY

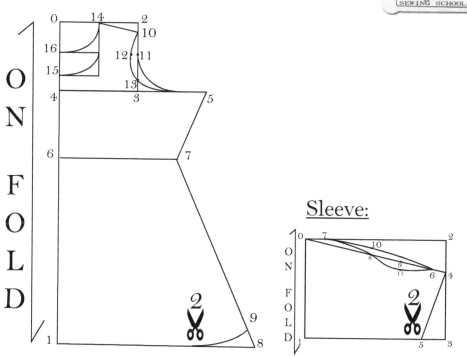

Sleeve:

Fabrics Required:

Kind of fabric = Printed Cotton, Kalamkari Cotton, Rayan Cotton

XS - S = 2.75mts

M - L = 3mts

XL - XXL = 3.5mts

FULL NIGHTY

MEASUREMENTS:

FULL LENGTH:

SHOULDER:

CHEST:

WAIST:

SEAT:

FRONT NECK:

BACK NECK:

SLEEVE LENGTH:

SLEEVE OPEN:

ARM ROUND:

WAIST LENGTH:

DRAFTING PROCEDURE:

$(0 - 1) =$ Full length + Seam allowance (1.5")

$(0 - 2) = 1/2$ Shoulder + Seam allowance (0.5")

$(2 - 3)(0 - 4) = 1/4$ chest + 1"

$(4 - 5) = 1/4$ chest + 0.5" (Ease allowance) + 1.5" (S.A)

$(0 - 6) =$ Waist length

$(6 - 7) = 1/4$ waist + 1.5" Seam allowance

$(1 - 8) = 1/4$ Seat + 5" /Fabric width

Join $(7 - 8)$ $\qquad$ $(8 - 9) = 1$"

$(2 - 10) = 1$" shoulder slope

Arm :
11 is the mid point of (10 - 3)

(11 - 12) = 0.25"

(3 - 13) = 1"

Neck :
(0 - 14) = 1/12 chest (Neck open)

(0 - 15) = Front neck + Seam allowance (0.25")

(0 - 16) = Back neck (2") + Seam allowance (0.25")

Sleeve:

(0 -1) = Sleeve length + Seam allowance (1.5")

(0 -2) = Arm round\ 2 + 1"

Square down from 2 and 1 and mark 3

(2 - 4) = 1/12 chest

(1 - 5) = Half Sleeve Open + Seam allowance (1.5")

Draw a line for (0 - 4)

(4 - 6) = 1.5"

(0 - 7) = 1"

8 is the mid point of (0 - 6)

9 is the mid point of (8 - 6)

(8 - 10) is 0.5" above

(9 - 11) is 0.25" below

Join (0 - 7 - 10 - 6 - 4) Back shape

(0 -7 - 8 - 11 - 6 - 4) Front shape

Stitching Flow Chart:

Step 1: Front neck design finish

Step 2: Back neck finish with cross piece

Step 3: Shoulder join

Step 4: Sleeve hemming

Step 5: Sleeve attachment

Step 6: Side join

Step 7: Bottom hemming

FULL GOWN

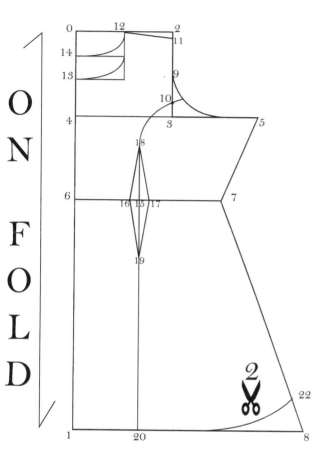

Fabrics Required:

Kind of fabric = Ikat, Raw silk, Printed silk, Georgette, Net, Chiffon

XS - S = 4mts

M - L = 4mts - 5mts

XL - XXL = 5mts - 5.5mts

FULL GOWN

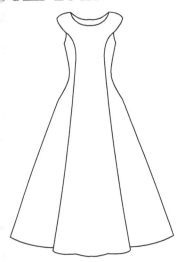

MEASUREMENTS:

FULL LENGTH:

SHOULDER:

CHEST:

WAIST:

SEAT:

FRONT NECK:

BACK NECK:

SLEEVE LENGTH:

SLEEVE OPEN:

ARM ROUND:

WAIST LENGTH:

DRAFTING PROCEDURE:

(0 - 1) = Full length + Seam allowance

(0 - 2) = 1/2 Shoulder + Seam allowance

(2 - 3) (0 - 4) = 1/2 Shoulder + 1"

(4-5) = 1/4 chest + 0.5" (ease) +1.5" (S.A)

(0 - 6) = Waist length

(6 - 7) = 1/4 waist + 1.5" Seam allowance

(1 - 8) = Fabric width

Arm :

9 is the mid point of (11 - 3)

(3 - 10) = 1"

Neck :

(0 - 12) = 1/12 chest (Neck open)

(0 - 13) = Front neck (1/8 chest) + Seam allowance

(0 - 14) = Back neck (1") + Seam allowance

(2 - 11) = Shoulder slope is 1"

Dart:

(6 - 15) is 4" from waist for front
and 3.5" from waist for back

(16 - 17) is 1"

15 is the mid point of (16 - 17)

(15 - 18) is 4"

(15 - 19) is 5"

Join (18 - 16 - 19) (18 - 17 - 19)

Draw a curve line from (18 - 10) and extend the line to 20

(8 - 22) = 2"   Join (20 - 22) with a curve line

Stitching Flow Chart:

Step 1: Join princess line

Step 2: Front neck finish

Step 3: Back neck finish

Step 4: Shoulder join

Step 5: Arm hole finishing with cross piece

Step 6: Side join and zip attachment for front placket

Step 7: Bottom hemming

FORMAL PANT

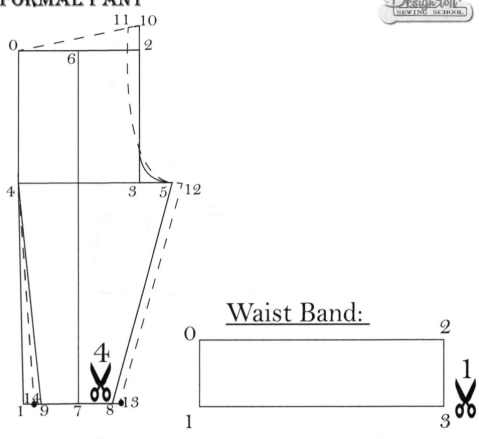

Waist Band:

Fabrics Required:
Kind of fabric = Suiting material
XS - S = 2mts
M - L = 2.5mts
XL - XXL = 3mts

FORMAL PANT

Measurements

FULL LENGTH:

WAIST:

SEAT:

BOTTOM OPEN:

DRAFTING PROCEDURE:

Front:

(0 - 1) = Full length + Seam allowance (1")

(0 - 2) = 1/4 Waist + 2" (Pleat)+ Seam allowance

(4 - 5) = 1/4 Seat + Seam allowance (1")

(2 - 3) = 1/4 Seat + Seam allowance (1")

(0 - 4) = Is same as (2 - 3)

(3 - 5) = 2.5" for shape

6 is the mid point of (0 - 2)

Draw a straight line and mark 7

7 -8) (7 - 9) = 1/4 of bottom open + Seam allowance

Join (4 - 9) (5 - 8)

Back:

(2 - 10) = 1.5"

(0 - 11) = Is same as (0 - 2)

(5 - 12) = 1"

Draw a curve line for (11 - 12)

(8 - 13) (9 - 14) = 0.5"

Join (12 - 13) (4 - 14)

Waist Band:

(0 - 1) = 5"

(0 - 2) = Waist round + Seam allowance

Square down from 2 and 1 mark 3

Stitching Flow Chart:

Step 1: Side join with front and back arrangement

Step 2: Side join on fly side

Step 3: Preparation of fly

Step 4: Zip attachment on fly

Step 5: Fly attachment on pant

Step 6: Waist band attachment with canvas

Step 7: Loop stitching

Step 8: Bottom hemming

CIGARETTE PANT

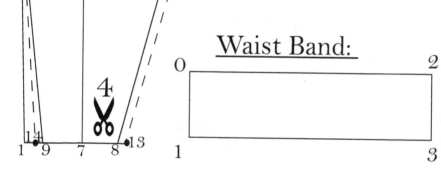

Waist Band:

Fabrics Required:

Kind of fabric = Cotton, Rawsilk, Silk cotton, Printed Cotton

XS - S = 2mts

M - L = 2.5mts

XL - XXL = 3mts

CIGARETTE PANT

Measurements

FULL LENGTH:

WAIST:

SEAT:

BOTTOM OPEN:

DRAFTING PROCEDURE:

Front:
(0 - 1) = Full length + Seam allowance (1")

(0 - 2) = 1/4 Waist + Seam allowance
(4 - 3) = 1/4 Seat + Seam allowance (1")
(2 - 3) = 1/4 Seat + Seam allowance (1")

(0 - 4) = Is same as (2 - 3)

(3 - 5) = 2.5" for shape

6 is the mid point of (0 - 2)

Draw a straight line and mark 7

(7 -8) (7 - 9) = 1/4 of bottom open + Seam allowance

Join (4 - 9) (5 - 8)

Back:

(2 - 10) = 1.5"

(0 - 11) = 1/4 waist + 2" + Seam allowance

(5 - 12) = 1"

Draw a curve line for (11 - 12)

(8 - 13) (9 - 14) = 0.5"

Join (12 - 13) (4 - 14)

Waist Band:

(0 - 1) = 5"

(0 - 2) = Waist round + Seam allowance

Square down from 2 and 1 mark 3

Stitching Flow Chart:

Step 1: Side join with front and back arrangements

Step 2: connecting both the legs by stitching middle round

Step 3: Bottom hemming

Step 4: Prepare waist band with elastic on back side

Step 5: Prepare waist band with canvas for front side

Step 5: Prepare waist band with canvas for front side

Step 6: Join waist band side

PALLAZZO PANT

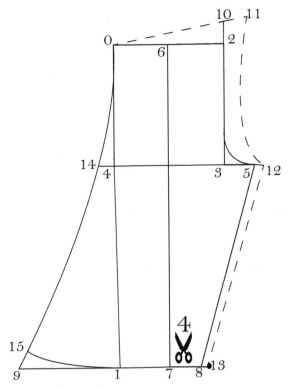

Waist Band:

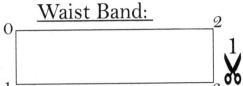

Fabrics Required:

Kind of fabric = Cotton, Printed Cotton, Kalamkari Cotton, Lissy Bissy, Italian Crepe.

XS - S = 3mts

M - L = 4mts

XL - XXL = 4mts - 5mts

PALLAZZO PANT

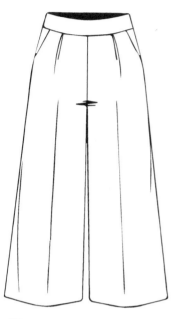

Measurements

FULL LENGTH:

WAIST:

SEAT:

BOTTOM OPEN:

DRAFTING PROCEDURE:

Front:

(0 - 1) = Full length + Seam allowance (1")

(0 - 2) = 1/4 Waist + Seam allowance

(4 - 3) = 1/4 Seat + Seam allowance (1")

(2 - 3) = 1/4 Seat + Seam allowance (1")

(0 - 4) = Is same as (2 - 3)

(3 - 5) = 2.5" for shape

6 is the mid point of (0 - 2)

Draw a straight line and mark 7

(7 -8) = 1/4 of bottom open + Seam allowance

(7 - 9) = Fabric width

(4 -14) = 2"

Join (9 - 14 - 0) with the curve line

Join (5 - 8)

(9 - 15) = 1", Join (15 - 1)

<u>Back</u>

(2 - 10) = 1.5"

(0 - 11) = 1/4 waist + 2" + Seam allowance

(5 - 12) = 1"

Draw a curve line for (11 - 12)

(8 - 13) = 0.5"

Join (12 - 13)

Waist Band:

(0 – 1) = 5"

(0 – 2) = Waist round + Seam allowance

Square down from 2 and 1 mark 3

Stitching Flow Chart:

Step 1: Side join with front and back arrangements

↓

Step 2: connecting both the legs by stitching middle round

↓

Step 3: Bottom hemming

↓

Step 4: Prepare waist band with elastic on back side

↓

Step 5: Prepare waist band with canvas for front side

Step 5: Prepare waist band with canvas for front side

Step 6: Join waist band side

FORMAL SHIRT :

Front:

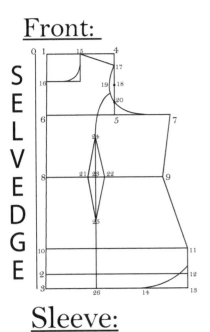

Back:

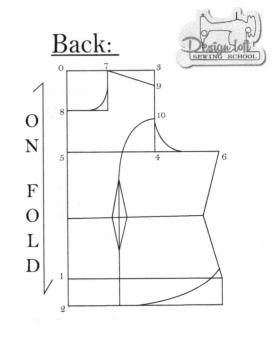

Sleeve:

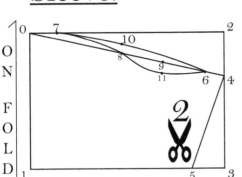

Collar:

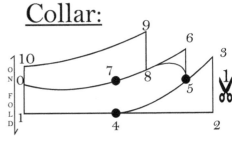

Yoke :

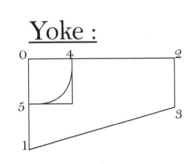

Fabrics Required:

Kind of fabric = Cotton

XS - S = 1.5 mts

M - L = 2mts

XL - XXL = 2.5mts

FORMAL SHIRT :

Measurements

FULL LENGTH:

SHOULDER:

CHEST:

WAIST:

SEAT:

FRONT NECK:

BACK NECK:

SLEEVE LENGTH:

SLEEVE OPEN:

ARM ROUND:

WAIST LENGTH:

DRAFTING PROCEDURE:

Front:

Place fabic selvedge over selvedge

2" for button and button hole placket

From selvedge mark as 0

(1 - 2) = Shirt length + Seam allowance (0.5")

(2 - 3) = 1" for Seam allowance

(1 - 4) = 1/2 Shoulder + Seam allowance (0.5")

(4 - 5), (1 - 6) = 1/4 chest - 0.5"

(1 - 8) = Waist length + 0.5"

(8 - 9) = 1/4 waist + 1" (dart) + 1" (S . A)

(2 - 10) = 2"

(10 - 11) = 1/4 seat +1"

(3 - 12) = Same as (10 - 1)

(12 - 13) = 1"

14 is the mid point of (3 - 12) + 1"

Draw a shape for (14 - 13)

Neck:
(1 - 15), (11 - 16) = 1/6 of neck round

(4 - 17) = 2"

Join (15 - 17)

Arm:
18 is the mid point of (17 - 5)

(18 - 19) = 0.5"

(5 - 20) = 1"

Join (17- 19 - 20 - 7)

Princess line:

$(8 - 21) = 3.5"$

$(21 - 22) = 1"$

23 is the mid point

$(23 - 24) = 5"$

$(23 - 25) = 4"$

Join $(24 - 21 - 25)$
$(24 - 22 - 25)$

Make a curve line from $(19 - 24)$

Extend the straight line from $(25 - 26)$

Back:
Fold fabric to the left side

$(0 - 1) =$ Shirt length $+4"$

$(1 - 2) = 1"$ for seam allowance

$(0 - 3) = 1/2$ shoulders $+ 0.5"$

$(3 - 4) = 1/ 4$ chest $- 1/2" + (3.5")$
now trace front pattern on the back pattern for
side line and bottom line

Neck:

(0 - 7), (0 - 8) = 1/6 neck round

(3 - 9) = 2" shoulder slope

Join (7 - 9)

10 is the mid point of (9 - 4)

Join (9 - 10 - 6)

Yoke:

(0 - 1) = 7"

(0 - 2), (0 - 4), (0 - 5) = Trace back shoulders and neck

(2 - 3) = 4"

Draw yoke shape.

Sleeve:

(0 - 1) = Sleeve length + Seam allowance (1.5")

(0 - 2) = Half of Front arm round - 1"

Square down from 2 and 1 and mark 3

(2 - 4) = 1/12 chest

(1 - 5) = Half Sleeve Open + Seam allowance (1.5")

Draw a line for (0 – 4)

(4 – 6) = 1.5"

(0 – 7) = 1"

8 is the mid point of (0 – 6)

9 is the mid point of (8 – 6)

Join (0 – 7 – 10 – 6 – 4) Back shape

(0 –7 – 8 – 11 – 6 – 4) Front shape

Stitching Flow Chart:

Step 1: Princess line joining on front

Step 2: Placket finishing with cavas on front

Step 3: Shoulder and yoke attachment

Step 4: Collar preparation

Step 5: Collar attachment

Step 5: Sleeve attachment

Step 6: Side join and bottom finishing

GAGRA :

Panel:

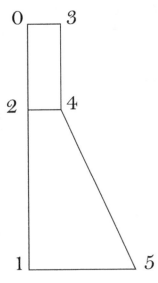

Waist Band:

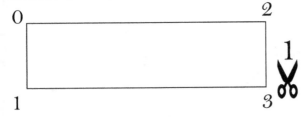

Fabrics Required:

Kind of fabric = Georgette,net,silk

XS - S = 4 mts

M - L = 5mts

XL - XXL = 6 mts

GAGRA :

Measurements:
Full length:
Waist:
Seat:

DRAFTING PROCEDURE:
Panel:

$(0 - 1)$ = Skirt length + Seam allowance $(3")$

$(0 - 2)$ = 8"

$(0 - 3)$ = Seat / Panel count + S.A $(0.5")$

$(2 - 4)$ = Same as $(0 - 3)$

$(1 - 5)$ = 2 times of $(0 - 3)$

Waist Band:
$(0 - 1)$ = 5"

$(0 - 2)$ = Waist round + Seam allowance

Square down from 2 and 1 mark 3

Stitching Flow Chart:

Step 1: Attach panels for front and back

Step 2: Cut waist size

Step 3: Join one side

Step 4: Attach with lining skirt

Step 5: Waist band finishing

Step 6: Side joining

Step 7: Hook and eye placket

Step 8: Bottom finishing

CROP TOP/ CHOLI :

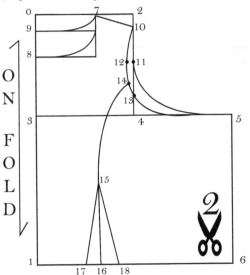

Sleeve:

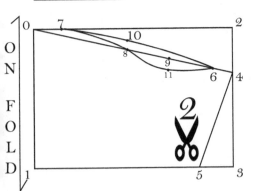

Fabrics Required:

Kind of fabric = Silk cotton,Raw silk,
                        Brocade,silk

XS - S = 1.5 mts

M - L = 1.75 - 2 mts

XL - XXL = 2.5 mts

157

CROP TOP/ CHOLI :

MEASUREMENTS:

FULL LENGTH:

SHOULDER:

CHEST:

WAIST:

FRONT NECK:

BACK NECK:

SLEEVE LENGTH:

SLEEVE OPEN:

ARM ROUND:

DART POINT:

DRAFTING PROCEDURE:

(0 - 1) = Top length + Seam allowance (1.5")

(0 - 2) = 1/2 Shoulder

(0 - 3) = 1/2 Shoulder + Seam allowance (0.5")

(2 - 4) = Is same as (0 - 3)

(3 - 4) = 1/4 chest + ease (0.5") + Seam allowance (1")

(1 - 6) = 1/4 waist + 1" (dart) + ease(0.5") +
     Seam allowance(1")

Arm :

11 is the mid point of (10 - 4)

(11 - 12) = 0.25"

(4 - 13) = 1"

Join (10 - 12 - 13 - 5) for front
(10 - 11 - 5) for back

Neck :

(2 - 7) = Shoulder width + S.A (0.75")

(0 - 8) = Front neck + Seam allowance (0.25")

(0 - 9) = Back neck + Seam allowance (0.25")

(2 - 10) = 0.5" Shoulder slope

Princess line:

(17 -15) = Dart point + (0.5")

(1 - 16) = 4.5" join (15 - 16)

(12 - 14) = 1" join (14 - 15) with the curve line as shown

(16 - 17), (16 - 18) = 0.5" each for dart

Join (15 - 17) , (15 - 18)

Sleeve:

(0 -1) = Sleeve length + Seam allowance (1.5")

(0 -2) = Arm round\ 2 + 1"

Square down from 2 and 1 and mark 3

(2 - 4) = 1/12 chest

(1 - 5) = Half Sleeve Open + Seam allowance (1.5")

Draw a line for (0 - 4)

(4 - 6) = 1.5"

(0 - 7) = 1"

8 is the mid point of (0 - 6)
9 is the mid point of (8 - 6)

Join (0 - 7 - 10 - 6 - 4) Back shape
(0 -7 - 8 - 11 - 6 - 4) Front shape

Stitching Flow Chart:

Step 1: Join princess line for front and back

Step 2: finish the neck line with lining

Step 3: Shoulder join

Step 4: Sleeve hemming

Step 5: Sleeve attachment

Step 6: Side join

Step 7: Bottom hemming

CPSIA information can be obtained
at www.ICGtesting.com
Printed in the USA
FSHW012247191221
87038FS

9 781720 286127